GEORGE SOROS

AN ILLUSTRATED BIOGRAPHY OF THE WORLD'S MOST POWERFUL INVESTOR

A COMIC BY **K**AORU **K**UROTANI

GEORGE SOROS

AN ILLUSTRATED
BIOGRAPHY OF THE
WORLD'S
MOST POWERFUL
INVESTOR

A COMIC BY **K**AORU **K**UROTANI
TRANSLATED BY **R**OB **K**OEPP

John Wiley & Sons (Asia) Pte Ltd

This edition published in 2006 by John Wiley & Sons (Asia) Pte. Ltd.
2 Clementi Loop, #02-01, Singapore 129809

Other Wiley Editorial Offices

John Wiley & Sons, Inc., 111 River Street, Hoboken, NJ 07030, USA
John Wiley & Sons Ltd., The Atrium, Southern Gate, Chichester PO19 BSQ, England
John Wiley & Sons (Canada) Ltd., 5353 Dundas Street West, Suite 400, Toronto, Dntario M9B 6H8, Canada
John Wiley & Sons Australia Ltd., 42 McDougall Street, Milton, Queensland 4064, Australia
Wiley-VCH, Boschstrasse 12, D-69469 Weinheim Germany

Library of Congress Cataloging-in-Publication Data:

ISBN - 13 978-0-470-82180-0
ISBN - 10 0-470-82180-9

Typeset in 9-18 point, Comic Sans MS and ComicsCarToon by Superskill
Printed in Singapore by Saik Wah Press Pte Ltd
10 9 8 7 6 5 4 3 2 1

TABLE OF CONTENTS

CHAPTER 1:
BREAKING THE BANK OF ENGLAND

Wednesday, September 16, 1992: The Bank of England is gripped by crisis

Pound Devaluation Unavoidable!!

Norman Lamont, Chancellor of the Exchequer.

Damn!

On this day at 8:00 in the morning, eight foreign currency traders huddle at the Bank of England frantically buying pounds in an attempt to support the currency's exchange rate band. The situation is bleak...

At 10:30, Prime Minister John Major is convening a meeting of senior officials who have gathered at the Old Admiralty Building.

Sir, there's a call for you from the Chancellor.

I'm afraid it's hopeless...

Yes. We've given up there.

There's nothing more we can do except raise our interest rate. Otherwise we'll have to withdraw from the Exchange Rate Mechanism (ERM).

So Germany's interest rate remains frozen?

3

At 11:00 the government announces that it's raising the interest rate by 2 percent.

This merely adds fuel to the fire. The markets become flooded with orders to sell pounds.

By 2:15 that afternoon when the government announces that it is raising the interest rate by a total of 3 points, the rate has appreciated 15 percent.

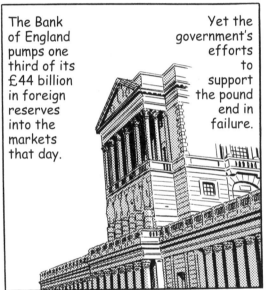

The Bank of England pumps one third of its £44 billion in foreign reserves into the markets that day.

Yet the government's efforts to support the pound end in failure.

The Bank of England is forced to concede defeat.

I see, there's nothing more we can do...

Alright then.

SLAM!

This is a day that will go down in history.

What about the Chancellor?

Hmmm...

I'll need to phone the leaders of France and Germany.

7:00 pm

Today was an exceptionally difficult day. Large volumes of money created chaos with the ERM.

The government has decided that the best policy to pursue is to withdraw from the ERM.

The Exchange Rate Mechanism, or ERM, was created in 1979 to stabilize economies of Western Europe in preparation for a single currency.

But with Britain's economy in recession, it became impossible to maintain the rate of 1 British Pound to 2.95 German marks as the ERM stipulated.

Afterwards people would refer to the events of that day in September as "Black Wednesday."

And one month later...

The Man Who Made One Billion Dollars on the Fall of the Pound!

The Daily Mail revealed the name of "the man who broke the Bank of England."

7

CHAPTER 2:
THE MONEY GAME

According to the Old Testament, mankind originally lived in paradise.

Without working, humans could have anything they wanted.

But because Eve ate the forbidden fruit of knowledge...

...humans were banished from paradise.

From then on mankind had to work to survive.

The 7th Century BC Greek poet Hesiod observed:

Because the gods are stingy with their blessings, mankind cannot escape from a life of toil and hardship.

About 10,000 years ago, people began cultivating agriculture. As they transformed the natural environment, they created cities.

Over time, nation states were born.

Between cities, commerce was conducted...

Markets that used monetary currencies developed.

In the early years of these markets, the wealth they generated was accumulated by men of political power.

There was no road to riches apart from acquiring political authority.

But once people were allowed to trade freely among themselves, men of wealth were created.

Regardless of social position or political power, one could enjoy a life of riches.

9

In Japan during the Edo period, rice was at the heart of the economy.

From around the nation annually taxed tributes of rice were gathered in Osaka. Brokers bought and sold the rice, which was then paid as a form of currency to local *daimyo* lords.

But the value of rice could experience extreme fluctuations based on the year's harvest.

So there emerged a system where in the spring, a price would be set to buy that fall's harvest at a fixed price.

This gave rise to commodity futures trading.

However, such trading was accompanied by risk. A bumper crop would send the price of rice plummeting, creating enormous losses for those who bought the futures.

Speculators willing to take this risk and buy the futures were indispensable to those who wanted to protect the value of rice.

10

In 1944, in the American town of Bretton Woods, New Hampshire; representatives from 44 countries gathered at an international conference to determine future monetary policy.

Britain and America argued over whether the pound or the dollar should become the principal global currency after World War II.

In the end, the American dollar won out because its worth was backed by gold.

The following year, the three leaders of Britain, the US, and the Soviet Union met at Yalta in the Soviet-controlled Crimean Peninsula.

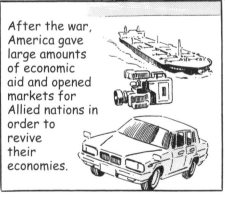

The Soviet Union was granted authority over countries that would be governed by socialism and the US granted power over those that would be governed by democracy.

After the war, America gave large amounts of economic aid and opened markets for Allied nations in order to revive their economies.

Moreover, to protect the freedom of the democratic nations, the US increased its military spending.

Eventually the value of dollars circulating clearly outnumbered the amount of gold for which they could be exchanged.

A great number of dollars were issued and flowed overseas.

11

On August 15, 1971, President Richard Nixon ends the convertibility of US dollars into gold. The post-war system for international currency exchange is destroyed.

With the demise of gold as a basis for valuing currency, the worth of currencies becomes entirely relative, measurable against a variety of other currencies: US dollars, German marks, British pounds, or Japanese yen, for example.

Markets thus become the determinants of currency value.

In this new environment where currencies are set by fluctuating market prices, a single hedge fund manager was able to speculate and win big.

He is George Soros. A master at his game, he has a Midas touch with his speculations.

CHAPTER 3:
SURVIVAL

George Soros[1] was born into a Jewish family in Budapest, Hungary, in 1930.

[1] His original Hungarian name is Dzjchdzhe Shorash.

His father, Tivadar Soros, was a lawyer and his mother, Erzebet, was a homemaker.

His older brother Paul—two years his senior— rounded out their family of four.

The two small provincial towns of Buda and Pest were radically transformed by successive waves of modernization brought on by the Industrial Revolution.

In 1848, the combined populations of Buda and Pest were 150,000. As of 1857, the number of residents was still less than 180,000. But when the two cities merged in 1972, Budapest had become a major city of one million people.

Viewed as outsiders, Hungary's Jewish population nevertheless had been making significant contributions to the foundations of Hungarian society by the time George was born.

Jews have traditionally made up about one-fourth of the city.

15

When George was nine, World War II broke out with Adolf Hitler's invasion of Poland on September 1, 1939.

Germany's powerful military machine rolled forward battle by battle.

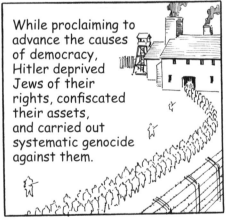

While proclaiming to advance the causes of democracy, Hitler deprived Jews of their rights, confiscated their assets, and carried out systematic genocide against them.

Because of Hungary's alliance with Germany as an Axis power, its Jewish population initially was spared from the evil of Hitler's designs.

In 1941, following orders from Hitler, Hungary's military joined the war under German command. The government of Miklosi Horthy sent its soldiers to do battle on the Russian front.

1943, a Hungarian state school.

You Jewish miser!

I'm only asking you to give back what I let you borrow!!

Shut up! You impertinent Jew boy!!

What the...?

It's a fight!

Come on George, let's lend a hand!

I don't get caught up in ethnic disputes.

Huh! What a chameleon.

Really... You'd never know he's Jewish.

17

19

At that time in Slovakia, anti-Jewish laws had been enacted and Jews stripped of their citizenship.

The Hlinka Guard, the Slovakia's equivalent of the Nazi Gestapo, sent them into concentration camps.

There they met with forced labor or mass slaughter.

Hungary became a of refuge for Slovakian Jews.

Dad, a police officer is coming!

Alright. Hide inside.

SHHHH

Are you Mr. Soros, the lawyer?

I am indeed Soros. Is there any problem with Hirsh here?

So you know this man?

He's a relative of mine from the Ukraine.

Ah, I see. He was carrying these items while loitering around the train station.

He certainly looked like a black marketeer!

Three days ago I sent you a postcard asking you to meet me at the station.

I never received anything. That's not unusual with conditions at the post office nowadays.

Hmm...

Since you went to the trouble to bring him here, please take this...

Oh my! Well...

Eh, eh. Mr. Soros, you're a real help.

We sure put one by that guy!

Policemen are people too. His reaction was predictable given the scarcity of food today. And we'd be out of an important source of food if you got caught.

Nowadays, even with food ration coupons, it's hard to get anything. You've always been there for us.

Well, I guess we are like family then!

HEE, HEE, HEE

HO, HO, HO

We have another guest from Slovakia.

For self protection, Hungary's Jews established an underground organization for hiding refugees.

As a lawyer, George's father provided aid and advice to many people involved.

23

George, are you still up?

I've been waiting for you to come back. Tell me again about what you did in World War I.

What am I ever going to do with you?! Oh well, I'll tell you until you get sleepy.

At the outbreak of World War I in 1914, the young Tivadar Soros was in the Austro-Hungarian Imperial Army.

Rising to the rank of First Lieutenant, he was captured by Russian forces and sent to Siberia.

In the POW camp, his leadership qualities were evident.

He was elected the prisoners' representative.

He also produced "The Wall," a newspaper that he wrote by hand to boost morale.

How long do we have to wait until the Revolution?

Mr. Soros

Last night, some prisoners from the neighboring camp escaped.

What? How many?!

It seems about two to three. They still haven't been caught.

I see...

All prisoners: come to attention!!

26

BANG!

Send out the search party!

Planning an escape?

No...

If you are, I want in.

As you can see, I'd be killed anyway.

GALLOP GALLOP

WHOAH!

Did you find the escapees?

Yes, sir!

SPLAT!

It seems they were attacked by wolves.

I see. Well, they saved us some work then.

Ha, ha, ha!!!

OH, HOH, HOH!!!

Damn!
So even if we make it out...

No.
There is a way!!

I get it. With this many men, the wolves won't approach us.

They had selected 30 prisoners for the escape; men with useful skills: doctors, carpenters, and hunters.

But at daybreak they'll send out a search party.

That's alright. There's a limit on how many they can send to look for us.

Moreover, now there's a revolution going on and Russia is in a civil war.

The search party won't want to run into enemy troops. They're not going to risk their lives to find us.

You're really something to have figured all that out.

Soros' group had successfully escaped from the camp.

But extreme hardship faced them in making their way from Siberia back home.

With the Russian Revolution of 1917, a new Soviet government was established under Lenin.

A town!

But land owners, capitalists, and others resisted. A state of civil war fought between the White and Red Armies persisted.

So dad, you and your men ended up fighting on both sides.

Of course, either Red or White. That was the only way we could survive.

And that way, Tivadar Soros lived to see the day he could return to his Hungarian motherland.

He went on to publish an Esperanto newspaper and become a lawyer.

Marrying Erzabet, the daughter of a rich family, he acquired a home and land.

34

OK. Now it's time for bed.

Although others might criticize his dad for now indulging in a life of ease, in George's eyes he was always a hero.

Good night, dad.

September, 1943.

DRRRRRRRRRRUM. DA DUM DUM

DRRRRRRRRRRUM DUM

Ahem!

What did they announce?

According to Regulation 270, by the end of the year all Jews in Hungary will be required to wear a yellow star sewn to the upper left of their outer garments.

Never!

They also passed a curfew. Jews are not allowed outside of their homes except between the hours of 10:00 am and 3:00 pm.

What is happening?!

I see what they're up to.

What is it dad?

You'll see tomorrow.

The next day.

It's no use, mom. After 10:00 am, there's nothing left to buy.

What?!

Food ration coupons are no longer any good for us.

This is unbearable! What have we done to deserve this?

This is war. In war, there are no rules!

So we won't be adhering to business as usual!

Let's play Monopoly!

Sunday, March 19, 1944: The Soros family is at their villa on Lupa Island.

What?! George has won again! What's the point in playing?

This game is too easy. I know, let's put in a stock market and add some rules!

Are you serious!?

NO WAY!

George, is it true your dad has sold this villa?

That's right. Once German forces arrive, our assets are going to be confiscated anyway.

It's best to convert what we have to money and food.

In any case, what's really valuable to us is what's contained in my dad's head.

My dad says the war will be over soon.

The Germans — what losers! Look at their defeats in Stalingrad and Kursk.

38

The Germans are here!

German tanks have crossed the Danube!!

So they've finally arrived...

At the time, Hungary had been secretly negotiating a peace treaty with the Allies.

Sensing as much, Hitler ordered his forces to occupy the country.

Then Hitler's representative and head of the Gestapo's Jewish section, Adolf Eichmann, came to Budapest.

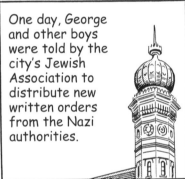

One day, George and other boys were told by the city's Jewish Association to distribute new written orders from the Nazi authorities.

What are we going to do dad? It says we are to gather at a school by 9 am tomorrow and bring blankets and a day's supply of food.

Your name is on the list, father!

Alright! Now it's finally happening!

These orders are for forced deportation. People have to be warned to escape!

Gotcha' dad!!

40

Yet even when warned, many chose not to do anything.

The law is the law. I am a Hungarian citizen. I obey the law!

Why don't people look at things realistically like dad does?

Assuming false identities, the Soros family went into hiding. So began a dangerous game of survival played against the German occupiers.

At the Soros' safe house.

Janos Kiss... This is my new name?

From now on you'll be the godson of Mr. Kiss, an official with the Ministry of Agriculture. You'll live as a Hungarian gentile.

You'll act as my husband's godson.

With that George traveled around Hungary with Mr. Kiss.

Their grim work related to the confiscation of property held by Jews being deported to Auschwitz — a concentration camp in Poland.

This is outrageous! What are you doing?

Be quiet! You Jews aren't allowed to hold any property.

Vacate these premises. Report to the Jewish Association by 9 am tomorrow morning. Now let's catalogue the assets of this mansion.

Stop!

Silence!

Uncle!

My, he's got quite a collection here...

If you don't get out by tonight you'll be sent to a concentration camp...

You're speaking Yiddish? Are you Jewish?!

You're a Jew just like us, yet you help others steal from us!!

CLICK

CLICK

What? Are you a Jew!

44

Huh?

Hah, hah, hah, hah, hah!

I get it. You've become multilingual to woo women.

But you better lay off the Jewesses. You'll just dirty yourself.

Hah, hah, hah, hah...!

47

I'm headed back to the office, go on home ahead of me.

What's happening?

The Jews are being put in a ghetto.

Oh!

BOUNCE

Mama. There's George!

George is Jewish. Why isn't he going with us?

So, a Jew. Show me your identity papers!

This is his passport.

Who the hell are you!?

Raoul Wallenberg, secretary of the Swedish Legation in Budapest.

A diplomat? Get out of my sight!!

Why are you crying?

Such awful things are happening...

I'm just so frustrated there's nothing I can do.

Things are as you say. But the war is almost over. You need to stay strong.

And never, ever forget what you're witnessing.

At the time, Wallenberg issued 600 Swedish passports in Budapest.

They were given out to save Jews.

The grounds of the Swedish Legation provided refuge to Jews and its personnel distributed food and medicine to the ghetto.

Even when threatened with being shot, Wallenberg would not shrink from his mission to save lives.

Finally in October, Soviet forces occupied Hungary. In December, an interim government was established under the Hungarian Communist Party.

Just as the war was nearing its conclusion, in January 1945 Wallenberg disappeared while on his way to the Soviet Military Headquarters.

It is said that he was imprisoned as a suspected spy and died of illness in 1947.

Ironically, the day after his disappearance, the Budapest Ghetto was liberated.

Then on April 4, all of Hungary was liberated from fascism.

Germany capitulated to an unconditional surrender on May 7.

The entire Soros family survived the Nazi occupation.

Soros' wartime experiences profoundly impacted his view of the world. The insanity of the era and its destruction of the orderly, comfortable life young George had known stirred in him an early questioning of authority and human rationality. This skepticism later would become a hallmark of Soros' deeply thought-out philosophy and his novel financial strategies.

His experiences also bred a compassion that Soros later channeled into his now well-known social activism and philanthropic activities. Although Soros was not actually saved by Raoul Wallenberg, the sort of humanitarianism and sacrifice that Wallenberg symbolizes is among Soros' positive inspirations.

More than anything, the survival skills he learned from his father, Tivadar, appear to have guided Soros in his mastery of global capital markets. Tivadar demonstrated a remarkable knack for reading "the big picture" in chaotic situations and doing whatever it took to "execute" the often difficult actions that were necessary to survive. Such traits likewise distinguish Soros' famed skills in reading the big picture of financial markets and making the large bets that other financiers either couldn't grasp the rationale for or simply didn't have the grit to carry out.

CHAPTER 4:
A JEW IN LONDON

1947: George Soros was in London.

Dad, I want to study at a university in England.

56

Dad! I got a reply. They've gotten me admission to an English school!!

I've got a classmate who's working for the political police. I can ask him to help you get a passport.

First I'll have you go with me to attend the International Esperanto Conference in Switzerland.

Then you'll go to Berlin by yourself and wait there for a visa to Britain.

Pay attention to world events and political currents.

We need to make war a thing of the past.

I made it
to London,
dad!

Two years
after the
end of the
war, Europe
was still on
the road to
recovery.

Following a war
that brought
destruction
and poverty,
London too was
in the midst
of rebuilding.

At the time, the failure of capitalism was seen as a major contributor to the outbreak of World War II. Faith in private enterprise had evaporated.

This involved nationalizing industry for the complex task of promoting a "mixed economy."

After the war, Britain's Labor Party came to power and tried to imitate the Soviet economic model.

THIS COLLIERY IS NOW MANAGED BY THE **NATIONAL COAL BOARD** ON BEHALF OF THE PEOPLE

In the midst of this, George worked part time to support himself in school.

GULP!

Heh, heh, heh...

RUMBLE

In 1948, London was struck by the coldest winter on record.

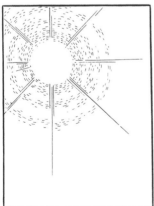

Lunnnch time!

Hey, is there meat in this?

Yeah, but it's rabbit meat. They didn't have the ration coupons for real beef.

Lord! When can we buy what we want again?

I hear that in Germany they've abolished rationing and price controls.

You don't say...

That ended the black market. Stores now are supposedly filled with goods.

Why don't they do that in England?!

You said it!

You really know your stuff.

You'll go far, kid.

George was studying at the London School of Economics (LSE).

LSE attracted students from all over the world. It was the perfect place for someone interested in studying applied economics.

At the time, LSE was home to such leading thinkers as Harold Laski, the socialist theoretician

There was John Meade, who went on to earn the Noble Prize in economics in 1977.

And the conservative thinker and later Nobel laureate Friedrich von Hayek, author of *The Road to Serfdom*.

Also Karl Popper, who came out with his monumental work *The Open Society and Its Enemies* in 1951.

An open society, no matter how unstable or risky, is forever superior to a closed society.

Popper's book had a profound effect on Soros.

You students base your appreciation of economics on laws and theories.

But you must understand economics scientifically.

SMILE

"Understand things scientifically," how can you do that?

As individuals, we don't all think and act alike.

Public opinions also can differ significantly.

Yeah, you're right. It's great to be able to share thoughts like this, isn't it?

You said it.

Say, let's visit the British Exhibition together.

The British Exhibition that year was magnificent. It demonstrated how the country was beginning to recover.

Do you mean he should get across town on his crutches and then climb three flights of stairs to get to this office?!

Don't you have any sympathy for his situation?

And so the money was sent by post.

In his studies, George wasn't reaching the goals he had set.

Damn. It's no good.

He wouldn't be able to teach in a university.

After graduating from LSE, he had to look for work.

His senior thesis, "The Burden of Consciousness," remained unfinished.

But its concepts inspired his business philosophy.

Several months later.

George, you're not really concentrating on the game. What's up?

I'm not cut out to be a salesman.

We've never beaten you once in Monopoly.

That's it, George.

After that, George wrote to all the City's investment banks.

He got interviews, but no job offers.

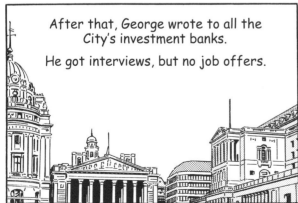

72

I see... Well, thank you for your time.

Just a minute. Let me give you some advice.

If you want to get into London's financial world, you'll have to change your technique.

Most of the people get in here through relations.

It's tough without connections.

Relations...

That's it!!

After that, he landed a job at Singer and Friedlander.

The managing director there was Hungarian.

There he became an arbitrage trader in gold and equities.

He gradually learned the business.

But at his age, he didn't have much by way of position or responsibility.

Hi, I'm Robert Mayer. I'm a trainee too.

Hi. You're American?

Yeah. I can't stand the food here. I hate this place.

Even so, things seem to be improving in Britain.

Hey, would you like to work in New York?!

My dad runs a brokerage. They're looking for people.

But I'm still just a trainee.

That's actually better. If we poached people with real experience they'd hate us.

You got a point there!

HA, HA, HA...

Hmm, New York...

Not having suffered the ravages of World War II within its mainland borders, America had grown strong by mobilizing its industries.

It was far more accepting of the capitalist market system than Europe.

The war had been a great destroyer of physical assets.

With industries that maintained their abilities to build and supply materials and products during and after the war, America was able to amass global wealth.

Its markets prospered.

Its economy continued expanding.

Soros decided to go to America. He applied for a work visa, but was rejected.

The reason given was that he was too young to qualify as an expert whose skills weren't already available from the US workforce.

George, I heard you finally got your visa!

That's right.

His employer asked Franz Pick, a major publisher in the field of arbitrage, to write a letter of recommendation for George.

He wrote quite a masterpiece... Arbitrage traders by nature must be young for the very reason that most die early from the pressures of their job!

Well, that's Wall Street for you, eh?

Say, didn't they have a lot die young in the 1929 Black Monday stock market crash?

It's just a joke. I'm not really going to die young.

It's ok. He's not in any real danger.

George, if anything bad happens, come back right away.

Promise me you'll take care of yourself.

OK. Thanks, I will.

But what about you two?

Let me know as soon as you've fixed a date.

What am I saying? You need to do things at your own pace.

What do I know about these matters?

Oh, George!

HA, HA, HA...

And so, George set off for America. There he truly found himself, developing his potential as a master in the arts of finance.

CHAPTER 5:
NEW YORK TRADER

1956: the Soros family reunites in America.

Dad, I see your survival instincts have been serving you well.

You boys have been doing well yourselves.

George's parents had come to America to escape turmoil in Hungary.

Paul, who had lived in France for a time, emigrated to the US and established a machine manufacturer.

In October of that same year, Soviet tanks rolled into Hungary to smash a democratic uprising. Tens of thousands lives were lost.

Prime Minister Imre Nagy was arrested and executed for treason. The spirit of the Hungarian people was deeply scarred.

So, how's work as a trader?

Right now I'm handling foreign arbitrage.

Arbitrage Trading — the buying and selling of stocks from the same company that are listed on different capital markets. Profit is made from the discrepancies between prices on the various markets.

It's strange but Americans won't buy European stocks.

Really, why's that?

American traders don't know anything about Europe.

I speak several European languages and am familiar with European companies and their owners. American traders can't even pronounce their names.

There were few people like Soros in the US who knew the European marketplace existed.

1957: six western European nations sign the Treaty of Rome.

The European Common Market is established for the purpose of expanding trade. The European economies revive, giving an upward lift to Soros' trading activities.

Soros developed "internal arbitrage"— trading different paper related to the same company, as opposed to stocks of the same company on different markets.

With his earnings and career growing, in 1959 he moved to the much larger Wertheim & Co., which was one of the few leading American financial firms that was active in overseas investment.

83

84

Merry Christmas, Annaliese.

Merry Christmas, George.

He was immensely happy with how things were going in life. But then...

In late 1962, word leaked that President Kennedy was planning to impose a foreign investment equalization tax, which would levy a 15 percent charge against the trading of foreign securities.

Soros! What's the meaning of this position you've taken in Tokyo Marine ADRs (American Depositary Receipts)?

The stocks are already in our corporate account.

If the ADRs aren't issued because of the new tax that will amount to a huge loss for us.

But I had the transaction approved in advance by the person in charge.

He denies he ever gave you any authorization.

What?!

But I know I...

That's awful. He said you lied?

It bothers me but there's nothing I can do. After all, it's a case of his word against mine.

George, I'm so sorry for you.

It's alright, as long as you believe me.

George!

A few days later, the ADRs were issued and nothing more came of the matter. But the new tax diminished much of the appeal of foreign securities and Soros' workload declined.

Later that year, George and Annaliese were married and George became a US citizen.

George decided to complete his thesis, "The Burden of Consciousness."

The days passed with him spending his free time working on his thesis.

He finally finished in 1963, sending the paper to Professor Popper.

Annaliese, he replied!

"Please come to the LSE to meet with me."

George, that's wonderful!

And so he went to meet with Popper. But...

What, you mean to tell me you're not American?

Why no, I was born in Hungary.

I see.

Is that so.

?

Popper had thought that Soros was an American. The notion that an American had been able to appreciate The Open Society had pleased him.

You have experienced German and Soviet oppression.

It's natural for you to see fascism and communism for what they are.

But what do you think about my thesis?

You've grasped the key points of theories well, but haven't taken them further.

You need to search for deeper meanings.

89

Only theories that can be empirically tested are scientific theories.

To create a great philosophical system requires truly original thought.

But you're still young. Take the time to carefully observe how changes in the world are occurring. That is the mission of a philosopher.

Thank you Professor Popper.

1963: Soros left Wertheim to join the firm of Arnhold & S. Bleichroeder. He spent the next three years applying himself to the development of his own philosophical thoughts.

Our understanding of the world is intrinsically imperfect.

Man's expectations and reality are at odds.

This contradiction enormously influences material development.

I will apply my theories to the marketplace.

The world will be my laboratory.

CHAPTER 6:
CHAOS

The firm of Arnhold & S. Bleichroeder was founded in the 19th century in Dresden, Germany. Many Europeans worked there.

The foreign investment equalization tax had destroyed the market for purchasing European stocks. Soros turned his attention to making money by selling the European stocks American firms had acquired back to European investors instead.

He then went into trading in US stocks...

First I want to establish a model account of $100,000 for the firm with 16 investment slots.

Each slot will be occupied with the shares of individual companies that look promising.

The reasons for the share purchases will be noted and a monthly report will be prepared on the portfolio's performance.

I'll then record our consensus views.

Using the model account for testing out new investment strategies, I think we'll be able to earn back a lot of business that we lost to the equalization tax.

The concept has merits.

An interesting idea. It's worth trying out.

How should we make our first purchases?

We'll buy stocks of the highest and lowest quality.

Then we'll observe their movements in price.

Based on those findings we'll expand our research on the stocks, solving any issues as we go along.

Congratulations. Your unit is pushing up the firm's performance.

What do you say to taking the assets from the model account to establish a fund?

Soros then created the First Eagle Fund, a mutual fund. It did so well that two years later he was able to establish a new fund, the Double Eagle, with $4 million.

Double Eagle was what is known as a hedge fund. A hedge fund is a private investment partnership that holds securities it believes are likely to increase in value and at the same time shorts securities it believes are likely to decrease in value.

I've put $200,000 of my own money into this fund.

Its clients are made up of aggressive investors from Europe, the Middle East, and South America.

The fund is established in Curaçao, part of the Caribbean Dutch Antilles.

This makes it exempt from requirements to report to the US Securities and Exchange Commission or to pay taxes.

But actual operations are carried out in our New York headquarters.

At the time, hedge funds of any significance essentially were limited to the one established by Warren Buffet in 1957.

Few people knew of these investment vehicles and almost no one really understood them.

The world's first hedge fund was pioneered in 1949 by economics journalist-turned-financier A. W. Jones.

Jones' novel idea centered around purchasing stocks, which were expected to increase in value, while at the same time "short selling" stocks from the same industry sector that were expected to decrease in value.

Positioning the fund for both "long" purchases and "short" sales amounted to a hedge against macroeconomic risks, facilitating an accelerated appreciation of capital.

Although Jones' approach to fund investment was admired, it did not catch on with other investment houses.

Jim! Jim Rogers, where are you?

Just look at this desk!!

Jim, I couldn't find you in the office. Where have you been?

There is nothing to indicate that markets behave according to a rational order.

This is because humans have at best an imperfect understanding of reality.

So, it is in fact a prevailing bias that investors develop from their imperfect understanding of the world that influences market fluctuations.

First, the bias produces a self-reinforcing upward pressure on the stock.

Market trends further bolster investor expectations. Trends and expectations work together to heighten upward pressure, over inflating the stock price.

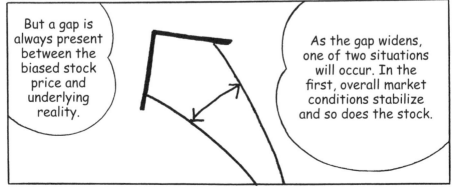

But a gap is always present between the biased stock price and underlying reality.

As the gap widens, one of two situations will occur. In the first, overall market conditions stabilize and so does the stock.

However, if conditions do not stabilize the situation gets out of control with investors losing confidence...

CRASH!

The stock plummets!

The key is to recognize the point at which the stock will crash.

Let's take this newly issued real estate investment trust (REIT).

It also appreciated in price at first. Then the price went too high and the stock was overinflated. In the end it crashed.

But that shouldn't scare you. There is a three to four year period before the bust cycle. Up until that point, we can safely purchase the stock.

The key is to hold on until just before the apex point, then we should sell.

Still, the rub is clearly seeing the point at which the stock will crash.

That's easy. I can always tell because my lumbago flares up.

HA, HA, HA, HA, HA

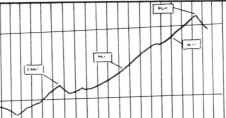

By short selling when the stock became over inflated, even greater profits could be earned.

As Soros predicted, while a stock price rose, huge profits could be made.

The chaos of the markets fascinates me.

It is within that chaos that money can be made...

What's with you, Jim? Aren't you feeling well?

I lost everything.

What?!

Several months earlier, when he anticipated a down market, Rogers took $5,000 of his own money to buy put options on machine tool stocks.

He then went and sold the put options at a premium of three times of what he had paid.

I tell you, it was superb timing!

Then the stock rallied for two to three months. I decided to sell it short.

I lost on that one. The stock is still going up.

... ...

Yeah, but aren't you glad you only lost $5,000?

It would have been much worse if you lost $50,000 or $500,000.

Hey, you're right.

If I look at it as the price for learning about the market, it's actually cheap!

RUMMMMMBLE

Whoah!

HA, HA, HA, HA

You can't do battle on an empty stomach. Let's get something to eat!

I'm with you!

Rogers was born in Demopolis, Alabama, a small town with a population of only 7,800.

He would go on to earn a reputation for his financial acumen and world travels, being dubbed the "Investment Biker."

Rogers graduated from Yale University in 1964.

In the summer he worked at the Wall Street brokerage of Dominick & Dominick.

He was then drafted and served for two years in the army where he managed the stock investments of his superior officers.

He obtained a graduate scholarship to Oxford where he studied Politics, Philosophy, and Economics.

After being discharged, he went to Wall Street with only $6,000 to his name.

Shortly thereafter, he joined Soros at Arnhold & Bleichroeder.

Although unsociable and prickly to most, Rogers got along with and admired Soros.

Soros likewise recognized Rogers' talent.

Together they formed a golden team.

102

CHAPTER 7:
THE GOLDEN TEAM

In 1973, Soros and Rogers struck out on their own to establish the Soros Fund with $12 million in investment capital.

Far removed from Wall Street, their office overlooked Central Park.

The split from Arnhold & Bleichroeder was amicable. Soros used the firm as the principal clearing broker for his new fund.

Investors in Double Eagle were given the option to remain in the fund or join Soros' new investment partnership.

It was a time of financial innovation. A formula for pricing options had been discovered, spurring the growth of derivatives trading.

The financial news service company Reuters had developed the "Reuter Monitor" which delivered real-time market information.

In the 1980s, the Dealing 2000 minicomputer was introduced, moving the financial world into the era of computerized trading.

The Soros Fund occupied an office of only three rooms and was run by Soros, Rogers, and a secretary.

Why are we located here and not on Wall Street?

First, because we don't want to have to deal with the high pressure environment of Wall Street.

Second, because we don't want to be associated with the herd mentality of Wall Street.

We have our own unique investment approach.

Third, apart from being different than Wall Street, we actually are better than Wall Street.

And fourth...

This place is close to our homes!!

The company reports you ordered are here!

Mail call.

Magazine delivery from Park Books.

Small parcel delivery, miss.

"Report on Hair Growth Treatments," "Understanding the Properties of Mint," "Fertilizers Weekly"?

What are these?

And we have hundreds of company annual reports!!

We use these to understand developments in culture, science, business, and government in order to spot new trends, identify emerging markets, and generate new ideas.

It's not just a matter of grasping company profits and sales. We use all these publications to see how society, economics, and politics will determine a company's future.

Children's Bookstore...

...delivery.

Uh, do I have the right place?

Of course!

Hey George, take a look at this.

It's a prospectus for a bond issue by an Oklahoma pipeline company.

They've taken out the provision that guarantees future supply of natural gas.

Now that's interesting.

Does that mean there'll be a shortage of gas in the future? Around where I live people are switching from using gasoline and coal in their homes because natural gas is cleaner and less expensive.

What do the sales reports of drilling equipment manufacturers say?

Shipment of drilling equipment has dropped sharply.

What does that mean?

Tulsa, Oklahoma.

The economy in this center for oil drilling is in horrible shape.

This is awful.

If things continue like this, America will lose its energy supply.

In the 1950s the government imposed price controls on natural gas.

Because of that, gas — which is given off as a byproduct when crude oil is extracted — was being sold at below the cost to produce it.

Accordingly, exploration for new natural gas sources virtually stopped. Gas production gradually declined.

Conversely, demand for gas increased because it was cheap and clean. Pipeline companies were reaching the limits of their ability to supply.

Have some coffee.

Thanks.

If the energy companies don't raise the price of crude oil they'll go bankrupt.

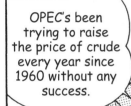

OPEC's been trying to raise the price of crude every year since 1960 without any success.

But I don't think the government is going to let things continue this way

... ...

The stock prices for natural gas drilling companies have reached bottom.

HMMM...

The fund went out and bought a variety of stocks from natural gas and oil drilling companies and from the major oil companies.

After that, by implementing export controls OPEC was able to raise the price of crude oil to four times that of its original level. Energy-related stocks soared. Soros and Rogers made an impressive profit.

HUH?

TEE, HEE

Is it true that Lockheed will file for bankruptcy?

The defense sector has been in decline since the US started pulling out of Vietnam. There's no war going on...

Hold it!

Last year the Yom Kippur War broke out in the Middle East!

That was when Egypt and Syria attacked Israel?

That's right. Until then the Israeli Air Force could boast of its undefeated record. But in this war the Egyptian pilots inflicted heavy losses on them. I wonder why?

Israel's military is supplied by the US.

Egypt and Syria are supplied by the Soviets. Maybe Israel's setbacks in the war weren't determined so much by people as by technology.

I'm off to Washington DC!

Will I get a bonus for this?

In Washington, Rogers met with Defense Department officials and other military experts.

111

He then traveled the US, visiting defense-related firms.

The reasons for Israel's setbacks in the war emerged.

Lockheed Corporation

Egypt's forces were equipped with the latest electronic technology from the Soviet Union.

Meanwhile, we've devoted our efforts to equipping US forces with conventional weaponry to conduct the Vietnam War. We've fallen behind in technological development.

But we can't afford to lose the arms race.

National security depends on our not lagging behind the Soviets.

I look forward to seeing how things develop for your firm.

By the way, who is Lockheed's strongest competitor?

That would probably be E-Systems.

AH HAH

Thanks.

The US government had to urgently address America's long-standing technological slide against the Soviet Union.

It would need to funnel money into America's defense industry.

Seeing this turn of events, the Soros fund took long positions on defense industry stocks.

Wow! Lockheed's stock has gone from $2 to $120. Another of our defense stocks went from 35 cents to $31!

E-Systems has jumped from 50 cents to $45.

I guess this means you'll be getting that bonus.

113

The Soros Fund recorded an astonishing 61.9% return in 1976.

As fund managers, Soros and Rogers were entitled to 20% of the fund's profits. Yet they ploughed the profits they earned back into the fund to reap even higher returns.

But it was not all good news.

The SEC, which regulates trading, announced that it was launching an investigation of Soros' trading practices.

Just before Computer Sciences issued new stock on October, 1977...

Soros instructed a broker to sell 23,000 of the fund's 41,000 shares in the company.

This caused the stock to depreciate by 50 cents per share and set a lowered price for the new issuance.

The day of the offering the fund purchased 155,000 shares. Later, to protect the share price, it purchased a further 75,000 shares.

Because of the price drop, the stock underwriter lost $1.5 million.

If we fight the SEC in court it will cost us time and money.

We're better off just paying the penalty to settle.

Without admitting nor denying guilt, Soros signed the settlement decree.

The penalty cost the fund $1 million. But having by then reached a size of $130 million, it suffered no significant loss.

Another matter had cost Soros dearly, however.

CHAPTER 8: SEPARATION AND REBIRTH

Oh, Mr. Soros, are you sheltering from the rain?

Ah, Susan. Yes, I've been caught in a sudden downpour.

Shall I take you to the subway station— or would you prefer a taxi?

... ...

If you're free, why don't we have lunch?

He bumped into 22-year-old Susan Weber that day quite by accident.

A graduate of Barnard College, she had studied art and after graduating was working on a documentary about an artist.

Soros had met her earlier at a party.

Actually, my divorce just came through today.

So please forgive me if I seem somewhat ill at ease.

I'm sorry to hear that... what was the reason?

My work. I was too busy to spend enough time with my family.

I didn't devote enough attention to my wife and three kids.

You manage a fund that earns an enormous amount of money.

If you can't enjoy your success, what's the purpose of your life?

You're right.

Up until now I've been too wrapped up in what I do. I need to change.

But...

But what?

It's easy to say but hard to do.

Heh, heh. At least you're honest about yourself.

I'll just have to take things slowly, step by step.

Earning money by itself is meaningless.

It's how you use it that counts.

Around this time, fund clients had been growing along with its profits.

Staff had to be added to keep pace.

But Rogers was against growing the company.

He kept overworking himself, shouldering the workload of four people.

It's hard for him to entrust responsibility to anyone else.

But there's no way we can grow the business otherwise.

Still, I've never had a partner I can work with as well as Jim...

Jim, we're reaching our limit here. If we continue like we have the workload will overwhelm us.

You have to build a team and let people below you share some of your responsibilities.

I'm gradually reducing my own work and looking for a successor who can later take over.

If you're to be that person...

That would never work. I don't have the skills for delegating. Even I know that.

In May 1980, Jim left the firm with a $14 million payout. The Golden Team of Soros and Rogers dissolved.

Since founding their company, the fund had not lost money in a single year.

By the end of the 1980s, the fund had grown by 3,356% to $280 million.

Afterwards, Rogers traveled the world on a motorbike. He logged 105,000 miles, earning a place in the Guinness Book of World Records.

Again in 1999, he set off for a three-year round-the-world tour in a yellow Mercedes, traveling 152,000 miles.

His journeys have earned him the nickname of the "Adventure Capitalist."

In 1979, interest rates in America rose from 9% to 21%.

Sure that if they continued to rise the US economy would suffer a major blow, Soros boldly took long positions.

He was betting that the Federal Reserve Bank would intervene to lower rates once the short-term rate exceeded the long-term. But the US economy went into recession and interest rates continued to rise.

The fund took a 22% percent loss. Some European investors began to pull their money out.

Soros visited his clients to explain the situation but it was tough going.

High return requires high risk.

It's the first time the fund has ever posted a loss.

Ironically, the US economy bottomed out shortly thereafter. Soros' prediction was early by half-a-year.

In September of 1981, Soros diversified his operations into a collection of funds and fund-related entities.

He gave control of fund capital to other managers and removed himself from daily operations into a more supervisory role.

Then in 1982 he married Susan Weber.

So, you're thinking of creating a foundation to fund charitable activities?

It will be a charitable lead trust that invests a fixed amount each year in public charities.

After that the remaining assets will be reinvested

What an idea!

I know!

I should use my wealth to dedicate myself to realizing Professor Popper's ideals for an open society.

In 1979, Soros had changed the name of the Soros Fund to the Quantum Fund, a reference to the uncertainty principle that underpins particle physics.

At the same time, he established his Open Society Foundation.

He had entrusted management of the fund to Jim Marquez and focused on his charitable activities.

But by 1984 the fund was lacking its original dynamism and losing top investors.

Soros returned to hands-on management in order to solve problems directly.

He thought of writing a book called titled *Real Time Experiments* to describe his investment philosophy.

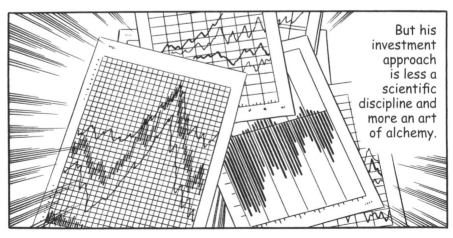

But his investment approach is less a scientific discipline and more an art of alchemy.

124

CHAPTER 9:
THE WIZARD AND THE APPRENTICE

When Soros did publish his book, he called it *The Alchemy of Finance*.

How do you find the book?

It seems to be filled with a lot of gibberish.

It definitely is difficult to read. Many parts are written in a literary style.

He talks about using a log of his trading activities as a real-time experimental laboratory.

But beyond this, the book seems to lack a scientific basis.

That's because he's actually using unscientific means to handle the uncertainty of the marketplace.

He made a major bet on the Plaza Accord.

The profits he earned in one week on that surpassed the total currency trading losses his fund had racked up over the past four years.

That also means he had to have the stamina to carry a loss for four years—I could never do that.

Again in 1985 he went long on the German mark and Japanese yen, putting in some $1.5 billion. That was twice the current size of his fund.

Yeah, he engaged in what amounts to high risk pyramiding.

Normally no one would ever do this. You could be wiped out if the trend goes against you.

But he felt the likelihood of that happening was small.

He believes that in free markets short-term interest rates will ultimately have to follow in line with the momentum of macro trends.

This might seem obvious now but he is amazing for being ahead of his time to recognize the new rules of the game in currency trading.

127

What he's trying to get across is that the market is imperfect. Whatever interpretation you can make of it is intrinsically flawed...

It appears you're using the wrong frame of mind to understand what he's saying.

... ...

If you can adopt his thinking, then no matter what happens...

you can manage to respond effectively to the chaos of the market.

Turner, do you know who that was?

No, who?

None other than Jim Marquez.

What?! You mean the manager that Soros fired from the Quantum Fund?

The young financial executive depicted in the previous panels is not the only person to find Soros' *Alchemy of Finance* a challenge. Yet the book, like the man's philosophical views upon which it is based, is hardly unfathomable. You have to approach Soros' writing with an open mind and appreciation that the language is intended to make you question your pre-existing views.

A key point for grasping the deeper meanings of *Alchemy* is to recognize that Soros refutes the idea that humans can accurately understand the world around them. Of course, just like the rest of us, even Soros is limited by an imperfect understanding of reality. His edge, though, is in knowing this. He then looks for whatever important stories are being ignored to capitalize on them. His string of successes shows that the philosophizing he does in the book hardly amounts to fanciful ramblings, but is in fact devastatingly practical.

A core concept in *Alchemy* is something that Soros calls "reflexivity." Reflexivity boils down to the idea that markets move according to self-reinforcing biased thinking that influences "not only market prices, but also the so-called fundamentals that market prices are supposed to reflect."[1] Reflexivity is what drives boom and bust cycles. Soros has made his fortune timing the reflexivity-driven peaks and valleys of the market.

[1] George Soros, The Alchemy of Finance (Hoboken, NJ: John Wiley & Sons), 2003: p. 5.

He was once considered Soros' successor.

In the end, Soros saw him as capable in executing but not able to go further in really understanding the market.

Stanley "Stan" Druckenmiller

August 1987: the Dow Jones Industrial Average continues riding high.

But Soros figured it was merely a matter of time before it took a dive.

Since Japan's stock market was more inflated than America's, he thought the bust should occur first in Japan. He took several billion dollars out of the Tokyo Stock Exchange and placed it in New York.

But on Monday, October 19, it was the New York Stock Exchange that crashed — Black Monday as it became known.

US stocks plummeted in value. Soros sold off shares in his fund's portfolio at a major loss.

Why would he do that?

Has he gone senile?

It might seem that way to some.

But no matter what others say, his actions saved the fund.

It's best to admit your mistakes and cut your losses early.

It takes real guts to be able to do that.

Several weeks later, using heavy leverage Soros went on to sell the dollar short.

It paid off. The fund ended up posting a gain of 14% for the year and swelled to $1.6 billion in size

What?

The Quantum Fund?

That's right. I've been invited to join George Soros' Quantum Fund.

Stan, does that mean he intends for you to succeed him?

So George, what kind of person is Stan?

Well, he was born in Philadelphia. He attended Bowdoin College in Maine and graduated with distinction in Economics and English.

Wanting to further his interest in economics, he was going to pursue graduate studies at the University of Michigan but he decided he wanted real-world experience instead.

He joined Pittsburgh National Bank in 1977 as a stock analyst.

In less than a year he rose to the top of the bank's equities research department.

That's something.

In 1980, he branched out to start his own fund. Six years later the Dreyfus Fund recruited him, where he served as its fund manager while still managing his own fund as well.

In 1987, funds under his management recorded the highest industry performance for the last 17 months on record.

That's great. He sounds like a good successor for you.

That's what I'm thinking.

But you've already gone through 10 or 11 people that you had considered as candidates to succeed you.

Don't you think you're being too difficult in your selection process?

No, I can't go easy on choosing the right person. Both for my sake and their's.

But Stan, all of Soros' chosen successors have not lasted very long.

I know.

In the worst case I'll get fired. But before that I'll have a chance to learn a lot from him.

133

Druckenmiller joined the Quantum Fund.

He tried to operate the fund on his own.

But Soros had never thought to give him complete authority at first. Instead he wanted to gradually hand over the reins.

Their work would bog down. The endless meetings and discussions wore on Druckenmiller's nerves.

Dear, are you alright?

....

Matters finally reached the boiling point.

SLAM!

What's the meaning of this?!

You sold off the bonds I had purchased without so much as a word to me!!

You were away from your desk. I felt action had to be taken immediately.

Don't you trust my decisions?!

I'm sorry. I won't do something like that again without talking to you.

Welcome home, honey.

The management frictions were to be eased by the tide of major historical events.

135

What's with you? I haven't seen you look so happy in ages.

Eastern Europe was in uprising. Communist governments were falling one by one.

In the fall of 1989 the Berlin Wall fell.

And Soros has his foundation offices set up throughout Europe.

That's right. He's desperate to get over there...

I'll be away for four to five months, Stan. The foundation offices need my support.

Please look after things while I'm away.

I know that I've meddled a lot in your work. While I'm gone I'll be out of your hair. Whatever you do in my absence, just be decisive about it.

The next five months are my big chance to prove myself!

Stan bet big on the German mark.

The country is running up huge deficits. It will be expanding its financial controls and tightening up lending. The currency has to appreciate!

He went long
by buying up
the equivalent
of $2 billion
in marks. But
the currency
continued
falling.

Stan! The
mark has
started
to rally!!

He had risen to
the challenge
and won! More
importantly, he
had won Soros'
confidence.

CHAPTER 10:
CREATING OPEN SOCIETIES

1980: Soros established a foundation office in South Africa. It organized scholarships for black students to attend the University of CapeTown.

80 scholarships were awarded but the foundation discovered that the money had been misappropriated. So the funding ceased.

The apartheid system is not easy to tear down.

Columbia University, New York

But our recent problems reveal weaknesses in our approach.

We have to ensure we have control over how the money is dispersed.

But weren't you originally opposed to getting involved in charity activities?

Our culture emphasizes the pursuit of self interest over the interests of others.

This is based on human nature and the principles of a competitive society.

Charities have the power to corrupt people. This applies equally to givers and receivers.

Many people exert more effort to finding ways to acquire money as opposed to doing what's right. The foundation needs to strictly enforce procedures to keep such people from receiving our aid.

Our foundation's activities are aimed more at groups or societies overall instead of individuals. We want to effect change on a large scale.

I see, so that's why it's called the Open Society Foundation.

Correct. We distribute money with a view toward building societies that allow freedom of expression and access to opportunities.

Soros chose his native land of Hungary to serve as a test case for the foundation.

Regarding the establishment of the foundation in Hungary... No foreigner has ever—well, in your case you of course are not really a foreigner, but the authorities there surely see you as an outsider.

And no foreigner has ever operated a charity in a communist country before.

Even in Poland, where despite the influence of the Catholic church, no charities have ever been established.

Except in Hungary today they're eager to attract foreign currency and credit from Western Europe.

The authorities are desperate to bring in hard cash.

So I'd like you to serve as my foundation representative there.

Soros had chosen the dissident Miklos Vasarhelyi.

Vasarhelyi had been the spokesman for Prime Minister Imve Nagy during the 1956 uprising. Following the Soviet crackdown, Vasarhelyi was expelled from the communist party and spent five years in jail.

141

In 1983, he was working at Columbia University's Research Institute for International Change.

The government will merely want to use your money.

I also want to use them. That's the basis of our cooperation.

My plan is to support causes by distributing small amount of cash in large quantities.

No matter how small, any self-governing organization serves to weaken the grip of totalitarianism.

It's as you say, Mr. Soros. Revolution starts one by one from the minds of individual citizens!

Then please work with me!!

In 1984, Soros and Vasarhelyi met with the person in charge of Hungary's economic relations, Franz Bader, to discuss establishment of the foundation.

Negotiations were difficult, lasting more than a year.

The Hungarian government only wanted support for scientific research. Soros wanted to support foreign travel and cultural activities.

The government decided to create a committee to work with the foundation.

Only plans approved by the committee's two co-chairs would receive support.

At last the day arrived when an agreement could be signed to establish the foundation in Hungary.

Whatever programs you want to implement just communicate them to our Department of International Cultural Affairs. They will handle everything.

Do you mean to say that the foundation would be under the control of the Ministry of Culture?

....

SLIDE

It really is unfortunate that all our work has come to nothing.

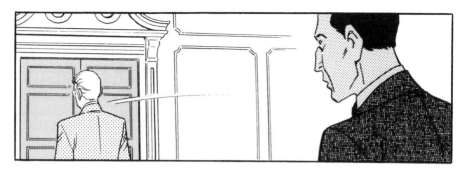

Wait!

Let's talk...

Unless the foundation can be self-governing this discussion is over!

145

You mean they agreed to that?!

That's right. Hungary is desperately short of convertible currency. They couldn't refuse when I told them I'd allow the $3 million per year that we will provide in aid to be converted at a level that is better than the official exchange rate.

With this the foundation was established. Yet the authorities watched it closely and prevented any mention of its activities from being reported.

However, through word of mouth people became aware of its work.

We need to use local currency, the forint, to distribute our money. I decided to take our nearly worthless forints and exchange them for photocopiers.

What?! Can you do that?

Until then, the government had limited the availability of copiers out of fear that they would be used to propagate dissident information.

At the time, the few copy machines in Hungary were locked up and required special permission to operate.

The foundation managed to give away 400 copiers to universities, libraries, and scientific organizations.

They were distributed under the condition that the government could not control their use.

The government considered shutting down the foundation. But the official in charge of overseeing it, Ferenc Bartha, refused.

He continued to quietly support Soros' goals from behind the scenes.

Along with its project for supplying copiers, the foundation supported a variety of programs that expanded benefits to society and promoted culture.

Information produced from the copiers spread throughout the nation.

The Hungarian government had intended for money from the foundation to support scientific research in the country and help appease anti-government sentiments in the scientific community.

But instead the foundation gave them money to study abroad. There they absorbed Western democratic values which they brought back with them to Hungary.

In 1988, a new government came to power and most of the communist leadership was replaced.

I never dreamed the work of the foundation would have such an impact. It's all because of you George!

I merely provided assistance. It was the people of Hungary who took the necessary risks to bring about change.

148

CHAPTER II:
BLACK WEDNESDAY

It began with the fall of the Berlin Wall in November 1989.

The people rose up to bring together the eastern and western halves of their country and forge a united Germany.

Unifying Germany has cost more than Prime Minister Helmut Kohl had anticipated.

Since 1987, the Deutsch mark has been Europe's principal currency.

Uniting two countries should incur enormous expense.

It means that the German government will have to be more concerned about solving the problems of the German economy than the fortunes of other Western European nations.

In 1990, Britain joined the European Exchange Rate Mechanism in the lead up to Europe's creation of a single currency.

But Britain's economy is weak. Its national policies are insufficient to allow it to successfully link with an economic power like Germany.

In 1992, the Treaty of Maastricht was signed by 12 European nations.

It created a unified economic structure. It stipulated that by the year 2000, all nations in the European Union would have a single central bank and a single currency.

To achieve these targets, the nations would have to maintain a single interest rate. This would further weaken the powers of currency speculators and traders.

But the signatory countries are not united in this. They still put national interests ahead of the European Union.

Accordingly, interest rates would have to be lowered if any member nations suffered poor economic performance.

But German officials were concerned about inflation being set off in their own country if interest rates came down.

There is genuinely deep concern that Germany's economy will falter and inflation set in. The fear of inflation is something that Germany cannot ignore.

Unless Germany agrees to lower its interest rates, other countries cannot lower theirs.
But if it does lower its interest rates, it will weaken its own currency— currency speculators will have a feeding frenzy.

The British economy had reached its low point.

In July 1992, Britain's financial leaders asked that the pound sterling's link at 1.6 Deutsch Marks be adjusted and interest rates lowered to 3%. The UK government ignored these pleas.

Countries lower their interest rates in order to revive a recessionary economy.

But the ERM doesn't allow this.

I wonder which will be the first to capitulate — British sterling or the Italian lire...

Soros built major positions in the British and Italian currencies.

1992

Let me once again make the government's plans clear.

We have no intention to devalue the pound and we have no intention of leaving the ERM.

Chancellor Lamont

And we haven't the slightest intention to reverse the progress we've made so far.

At that time the Bank of England poured the equivalent of £3 billion into the market to support the sterling's peg at 2.778 Deutsch Marks.

At what level do you want us to come in?

153

I'm thinking we should come in at $4 billion.

No, we'll need more than that.

When you think you're right to come in, you have to come in with maximum force.

Helmut Schlesinger, the president of Germany's Bundesbank, claims he's behind the concept of a single European Currency Unit (ECU). Yet he's really only interested in promoting one existing currency to create it.

You mean he's only interested in the fate of the mark.

If the Bundesbank doesn't maintain the current fixed exchange rates for the mark, Germany's economy will be in peril.

There are indications that the lira is especially weak.

First we'll short the lira. If it depreciates, downward pressure on the pound will increase.

So with only $1 billion as collateral, they borrowed $3 billion to then take a $10 billion position.

The fall of the ERM will set off a chain reaction.

Plans for the ECU will have to be restructured. Interest rates will fall and stock markets will decline.

First we will short the currencies and then bet on the bond and stock markets.

We'll short the pound at the level of $7 billion and go long on the mark at the level of $6 billion. At a lesser amount we will go long on the French franc.

I see a country's stock market rising after depreciation of the currency, so while shorting the pound I'll buy up $500 million in British stocks.

If the mark appreciates German stock values will decline but bond values will increase.

So we'll go long on German and French bonds and short German and French stocks.

After the necessary pieces were in place, they had only to wait for the storm to follow.

September 1: mutual funds and multinational corporations start selling off the weaker European currencies.

Trading activity is picking up.

I don't know who is going to have enough capital reserves to support these currencies.

September 3: Chancellor Lamont announces plans to borrow £7.5 billion from international financial institutions in order to support the sterling.

That should take care of things.

It looks like Lamont was able to pull it off.

September 10: Prime Minister Major speaks at an industry federation conference in Glasgow.

Britain will never choose to instigate inflation by devaluing our currency and lowering our interest rates.

YEEEEH!

Rumors circulate that the Italian Lira is about to be devalued

Sell, sell!!

We've got to sell lira before it falls!!

September 13: the lira is devalued by 7% but this is still within the parameters of the ERM.

Until now the central banks of European governments have been frantically buying their own currencies in order to maintain existing exchange rate levels. But there is a limit to how far they can go...

The lira's falling again!

Buy marks!!

Tuesday, September 15

Sterling, sell pound sterling!!

The Bank of England is stepping in to buy £3 billion to prop up the pound.

But it's no good, the pound can't hold ground!!

The Bundesbank announces that it is cutting its official discount rate by 0.5%. But sterling falls to 2.778 marks, its lowest level since Britain joined the ERM.

London and New York are separated by a five hour time difference.

The fireworks have yet to begin.

We're ready.

The fateful day of Wednesday the 16th arrives.

Pound Devaluation Imminent!!

The Wall Street Journal publishes damaging remarks made by Bundesbank's Schlesinger.

Speculators go into a frenzy of dumping lira and pounds and buying up marks

Sell, sell!!

Sell pounds!!

Sell it!

11:00 am

Lamont just announced he's raising interest rates by 2%!!

It's no good, the pound won't go up!!

Game over...

WHOOOOOOOOOOOAH

After that the government raised the interest rate a further 3% to 15%. The pound continued to slide.

Prime Minister Major was forced to concede that the UK would leave the ERM. Following Britain, Italy left the ERM as well.

Thus was brought down the Bank of England, a symbol of British power and prosperity.

The day became known as Black Wednesday.

Then on October 24, *The Daily Telegraph* newspaper delivered a second shock to the British people!

The Man Who Made One Billion Dollars on the Fall of the Pound

Soros?

Who's he?

George Soros?

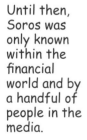

Until then, Soros was only known within the financial world and by a handful of people in the media.

But from this moment forward he would be widely known as "the man who broke the Bank of England."

161

Those in government circles were unanimous in their condemnation of Soros.

He's destroyed the dream of European unity!!

His cost to the British taxpayers is £25 per person.

But he was mainly seen as a hero to the people.

It takes quite a guy to make a fool of the government.

A modern day Robin Hood.

The total £4 billion the government lost trying to prop up the pound was more than the cost of participating in the Gulf War!

What kind of idiots do we have in government?

Soros was admired while the bank and government were derided for their incompetence.

With the pound devalued, imported goods will become cheaper and more plentiful.

That actually is positive for the economy.

That year, Soros became known as the most profitable man on Wall Street.

His fund grew by 68% over the previous year and rose to $3.7 billion in capital.

But there was a flip side to this good fortune.

Apart from Soros, many speculators and funds suffered heavy losses from the fall of the pound.

Even though this is to be expected in currency speculation, concerns about the repercussions of Black Wednesday grew.

A movement got under way in the US Congress and within central banks to add regulatory controls.

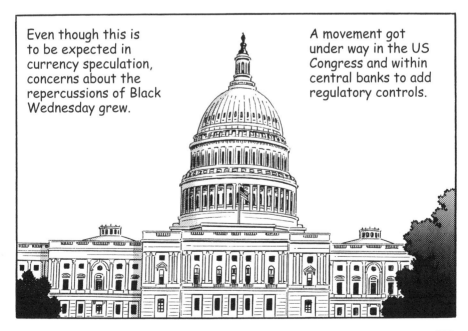

CHAPTER 12:
PUBLIC HEARING

With you becoming so famous, that's bound to help the expansion of the foundation.

Now politicians all over the world seek me out.

The foundation has blossomed as a network of organizations operating in more than 20 countries.

But this also meant that governments more closely monitored his movements.

Many people wanted to ride on his coattails.

His words could now move markets. The amount of money used in speculations rose.

On February 11, negotiations had broken down between the leaders of the US and Japan to solve trade issues that favored Japan.

On February 14, 1994, Soros lost $600 million betting against the Japanese yen.

When the markets in New York opened three days later on Monday, the yen suddenly shot up 5%.

But Soros' losses amounted to only 5% of his fund's assets.

Other funds also lost money. To compensate, they redeployed their capital to purchasing yen or stocks from Japan and Europe.

The problem was the chain of events the yen's appreciation caused.

This created chaos in the European markets.

There was a movement to regulate derivatives trading and crack down on illegal activities in financial markets.

The US Congress viewed these events with concern. It convened public hearings where Soros and other funds were investigated.

166

In principle, we are unable to accurately foresee the future direction of markets.

But there is influence you can observe from economic fundamentals.

The market creates its own momentum according to the upward and downward movements of the business cycle.

Trading activity becomes biased toward these trends. This will lead to the market crashing when things head downward.

So what is it that creates these self-reinforcing market trends?

Mutual funds and institutional investors are a major factor.

They don't focus on the intrinsic value of the financial products they handle. They're only concerned about maintaining a performance relative to the market.

It becomes such that everyone is merely following everyone else.

167

Hedge funds are also a factor. But we represent only 0.005% of the currency volume traded.

What do you mean by hedge funds?

Our purpose is to hedge against risk.

Usually we operate in the opposite direction of the trends followed by institutional investors.

In this sense you could say we help correct volatility in the marketplace.

Have you manipulated currency markets?!

No speculator is capable of that.

Our fund's daily trading volume is at the level of $500 million.

The foreign exchange market's daily transaction volume is $1 trillion. The difference is an order of magnitude.

What about derivatives trading?

My funds are adequately supported by their investors. We have no reason to issue or broker derivative instruments.

Moreover, there are so many different varieties of derivatives and they're not easy to understand. It makes managing their risk difficult.

I have my doubts about any financial instrument that does not pay off according to its principal structure

Yet I believe the government's and the market's interests will be at odds if you try to regulate derivatives.

You can expect fierce resistance from the marketplace.

A Governor of the Federal Reserve Bank

In regards to domestic banks, they only allocate 0.2% of their assets to derivatives trading.

A Commissioner from the SEC

Hedge funds currently are covered by laws governing banks and securities.

We don't wish to increase regulation in this area...

We would like them to be more open about their trading activities, however.

The real issue boiled down to the government being unable to track the investment movements of hedge funds.

We allocate 60% of our fund capital for direct trading. This is enough to cover most of our stock purchases without needing to use additional credit.

Another 20% we leverage for speculative macro-based trading in currencies and stocks.

The remaining 20% is used for trading on credit. It is invested in short-term treasury bills and bank depository notes.

It's said that hedge funds like yours make illegitimate profits.

We always follow the law when we speculate. Making profit from our speculations is our job.

Congress and the press generally viewed Soros' testimony favorably. He left Washington unscathed.

It's good things turned out alright.

I never thought they wouldn't.

Yet I understand the public's concerns.

Anything that people create is imperfect.

Rules and markets have flaws, and we exploit them to make our money.

So long as markets develop and expand, elements of risk are sure to proliferate as well.

But there's no way to control it.

That's right. Just as in life, control is impossible.

Exactly how one should deal with this uncertainty...

I constantly wonder it about myself.

Chapter 13:
Trends and Risks

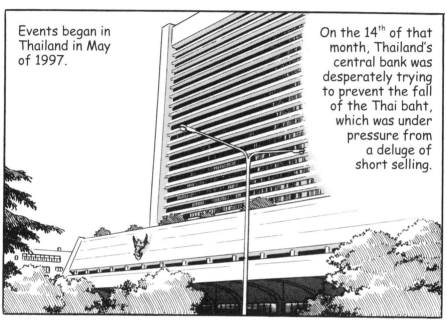

Events began in Thailand in May of 1997.

On the 14th of that month, Thailand's central bank was desperately trying to prevent the fall of the Thai baht, which was under pressure from a deluge of short selling.

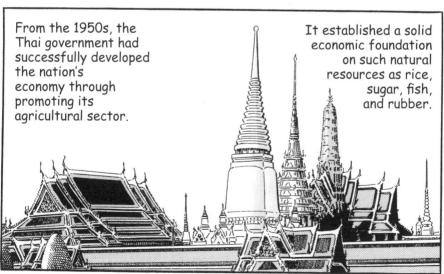

From the 1950s, the Thai government had successfully developed the nation's economy through promoting its agricultural sector.

It established a solid economic foundation on such natural resources as rice, sugar, fish, and rubber.

With the immense economic demands generated by the nearby war in Vietnam, Thailand's economy boomed.

At the time of the second oil shock, Thailand adopted a currency peg for the baht which tied it to the US dollar.

After the Plaza Accord came into effect in 1985, the value of the dollar declined.

With the attendant lowered cost of Thai produced goods, the country's manufacturing competitiveness increased. The economy industrialized.

In the 1980s, money from Japan poured in to fuel the expansion, creating the beginnings an economic bubble.

The rapid development of the economy also fueled corruption and oversupply of goods.

Foreign debt in Thailand has swelled to $80 billion.

The government is making plans to restructure the worsening economy.

Financial institutions there are already contending with over 10% of their assets being made up of bad debt.

The time is not far off before the baht will have to devalue.

I was thinking of gradually short selling the baht to see what happens.

From early 1997 major bankruptcies started occurring.

Rumor spread that the baht would have to be devalued.

Then on May 14, there was a flood of short selling the baht.

To support the currency, the Bank of Thailand asked for emergency financial assistance from other countries.

At the same time it took extreme measures, raising the lending rate from an already high 25%.

Now they're raising the lending rate from 500% to 1,000%.

The rate has hit 3,000%!

The Bank of Thailand has really responded hard. We can't match them.

It's a temporary setback. They can't maintain such extreme policies.

Our chance will come.

Thailand had been using massive amounts of dollars from its foreign currency reserves to prop up the baht. But those reserves were dwindling, which was eroding the government's ability to make payments on Thailand's foreign debt.

As Soros predicted, there was a change in government. The new leadership exacerbated the situation.

Friction developed within central government departments. The prime minister asked for the resignation of the finance minister.

The chaos finally brought about the demise of the currency peg on the morning of July 2.

It's a sell off!

The whole world is dumping their baht holdings!

... ...

On this day the currency dropped 15% against the dollar and the government announced that it had abandoned its peg.

The currency crisis spread throughout Asia. Approximately 30 million people became unemployed as a result.

177

In October, owing to currency volatility the Hong Kong Stock Exchange plummets!!

Because of a fail safe mechanism in the trading system, the exchange is able to avert disaster.

Korea also became a victim to the continuing chain reaction.

Korean banks had large amounts of loans denominated in yen. They also were active in bond trading throughout Asia.

When the Asian markets fell, the amount required to pay off short term loans swelled to $15 billion.

Korea thus sold off foreign assets it held to make its payments.

Among these were a large number of short-term government bonds issued by Russia.

At the time the Russian government had issued massive amounts of short-term bonds to cover its fiscal deficit. Most of the purchasers were foreign investors.

Having failed with economic liberalization, Russia issued bonds at interest rates that were exceptionally high in order to cover for its runaway inflation. The extraordinary interest rates brought in foreign capital.

But now in order to cover losses caused by speculation activities in Asia, Russian bonds were being sold off en masse. The prices of Russian bonds and stocks fell as a result.

Foreign investors in Russia began pulling out their money.

On August 17, 1998, Prime Minister Sergei Kiriyenko asked foreign bond holders for a three month moratorium on Russian interest payments.

The government announced a suspension to the issuance of new short-term government bonds and imposed currency exchange controls. Russia's capital markets were thrown into turmoil.

This sent shock waves throughout the world's financial community. Many had poured large amounts of investment into Russia and their losses were mounting.

Soros' funds were no exception.

Originally the Open Society Foundation had a policy that any country, such as Russia, where the foundation had an office, Soros-affiliated funds would not make any investments.

Yet as the capital markets of Eastern Europe developed, that rule became impractical. His funds began investing there as well as in Russia.

Many other sizable hedge funds followed in Soros' wake.

Long Term Credit Management (LTCM), run by a fund management "dream team" that included a Nobel laureate economist, lost 40% of its fund capital.

The heads of major American banks that had invested in LTCM gathered together and decided to bail out the fund.

They were afraid that the failure of LTCM would create panic in the global financial markets.

181

I may just be a failed philosopher...

But there's a lot of work left to do.

At this point Soros effectively handed over management of the Quantum Fund to Druckenmiller and dedicated himself to working on projects at the foundation.

He established universities and scholarships.

During the Bosnian conflict he teamed with Fred Cuny and helped the citizens of Sarajevo by installing water-purifying facilities.

He created the International Science Foundation which has aided Russian scientists. Some 35,000 individuals have received monetary support from the foundation.

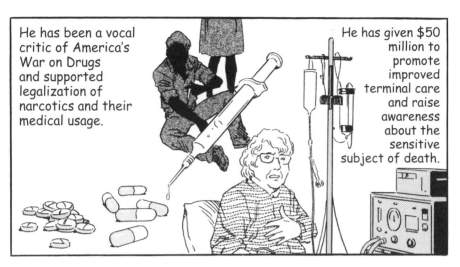

He has been a vocal critic of America's War on Drugs and supported legalization of narcotics and their medical usage.

He has given $50 million to promote improved terminal care and raise awareness about the sensitive subject of death.

From 1994 until 2000, his various foundations and initiatives have dispersed more than $2.5 billion.

Making money is easy, the hard thing is spending it well.

I couldn't live with myself if I felt I hadn't given anything back to society.

With the bursting of the bubble for Internet-related stocks in 2000, the Quantum Fund—which at its height had $22 billion in assets—lost $7.6 billion.

Druckenmiller decided to step down from the fund, making its closure inevitable.

Based on information posted on the Internet, after the 9-11 terrorist attack on the World Trade Center, Soros is alleged to have taken major positions short selling American stocks, bonds, and the dollar in foreign capital markets

When US markets opened a week later to large losses, he is said to have earned as much as $15 billion.

In the 2004 US presidential election he was again in the spotlight as a major contributor to President George Bush's opponent, John Kerry.

And so he continues in his quest to make "Open Societies" a reality.

Where to go for investment success

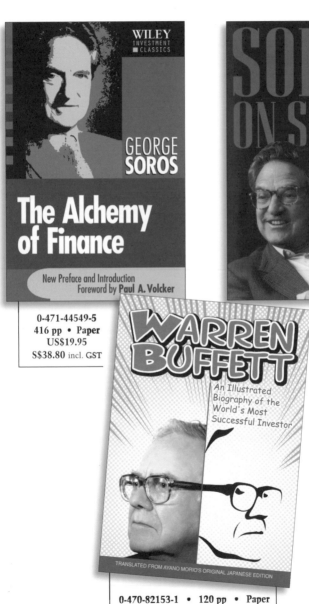
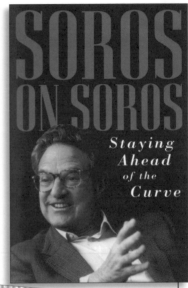